Literary production
IL MELETO

Elia Bardinero

The Way

Dō

A book about the *Way*

IL°MELETO

Title: The Way
Author: Elia Bardinero
[*Pseudonym of* Giuseppe Costa]
(Bibliography p. 67)
(Biography p. 68)

September 2019

ISBN 979-12-200-5396-9

GENERAL INDEX

*The mind organizes strategies
for attacks and defences of all kinds.
The art of living is the art of fighting.
We were born to fight and to succumb.*

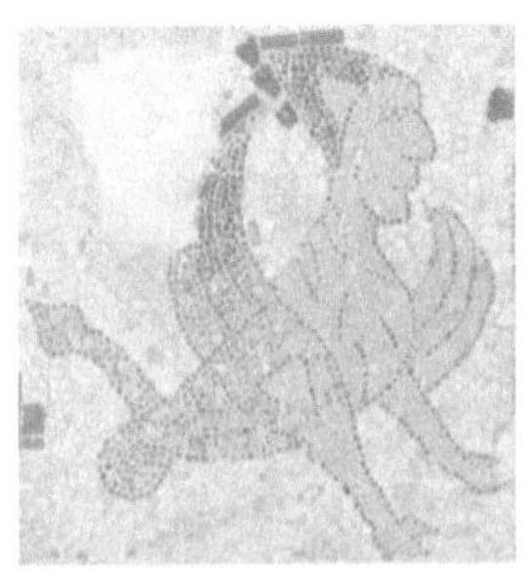

THE WAY

The method in Zen practice

Have a good path in the Way!

Nam myōhō renge kyō

Beginning

The continuous, urgent, insistent search, led me to give in to the conviction that the meaning of life and of actions is part of a reality which intellect alone cannot penetrate. The final purpose cannot come into view. So that the deepest knowledge, which lacks the proof of the senses and of a language which is able to describe it, refers to experiences that hint at the implicit values of that awareness-filled sensitive space.

The intellect, anyway, must move the first step. It must observe the world looking beyond fascination and appearances, leaving more and more space to the listening rather than to the words and the thoughts, and must serve that true which has no voice nor face, but that appears in the simple being ourselves, in the bright space of a no longer lost mind, beyond the sphinxes of the enigmas of life.

Elia Bardinero

"Ensō con autoritratto nelle vesti di sōhei"
(僧兵, letteralmente "monaco soldato")

Esecuzione di Ou An Sensei
(fernando lembo di Pino)

The Way among the waves

The Way is more similar to the sea,
Restless, without paths nor tracks.

Walking the Way is like being on the high seas, among the waves, far away from the shore that we occasionally think to see, with the doubt that it might not be the actual shore we need to reach, or whether the end should be a shore or an endless sea. We go on in the hope of getting to authentic goals; of landing, maybe in the moment a wonderful dawn is showing, on a pink beach, or, who knows, in the coolness of the leaves, in an evening full of fresh air and of fireflies, finally far from this endless effort; far from this persistent lament, from this constrained interrupted breath.

Definition of Way

The instruction of the Way is not the Way.
Following the instruction is the Way.

Proceeding correctly along a Way, involves a deeply felt sharing of the declared principles and a disposition to that kind of discipline so that the progress in the field of a specific perfection course would also depend on preexistent conditions, which are likewise at the base of the pleasure of practicing and of the growing satisfaction for the achieved results.

Often the motivations of those who undertake a training, concern the desire of personal success or advantages, with time and patience for a good practice, the beauty of a different dimension of being will appear under a new light, this beauty will be surrounded by a thinner and more careful kind of listening and by a maturation towards a nature which is more bound to exclude the illusory line between the I and the other.

Those initial reasons will tend to an interior vision and to a different nature of the self; to that hidden and unknown part brought to light, step by step, by gradual conquests along the fantastic path of the practice. In this way we can get closer to the horizon of the Way, to the limit of the abyss, to that Borderland towards the highest experience of the fall, of the sudden, unexpected change.

The Way and its aim

The purpose of the practice of the Martial Art or Zen practice, should be that to obtain, through the balance and the art, the best efficacy of the action, keeping alive, at the same time, the originality of the teachings and the opportunity to raise to a mental state of Clear Vision that they offer becoming this way a tool of introspection for a better and true sight of ourselves and of the world.

The noble purpose of the Way seems to be realizing in depth the rules of a way of acting that uncovers our true nature, so that the spontaneous and creative part of it can be grasped enough for us to wonder about its correctness and legitimacy and about our intentions.

Attaining a True Technique is the tool that makes us masters and responsible of our actions, even beyond our inborn knowledge.

The right Way

JUTSU
The Way and the Technique

The technical knowledge, like any other kind of knowledge of the rules, is mastership of the environment and of the natural balances which donate to the rules themselves legitimacy and value. Ethic and a good level of awareness are generated and depend on such knowledge, with whom, based on its grade, is possible to verify the more or less correct application of these notions and to deepen the search, to understand the moral meanings that each True Technique has in itself, for the natural aspiration to the harmony and the art.

The destination of the Way

The horizon of the Way
The borderland

Along with the understanding, which derives from the experience of the correct application of the law, the conviction that the Way through the art concerns ethic and its values, can be strengthened. In the same way it is more and more evident how the sense of rules and discipline shines through, and how rules and discipline themselves are closely connected to the naturalness of the method.

Art, ethics and technique get together and strengthen each other reciprocally until they reach a comprehension that transcends the physical fact, towards the vision of a reality otherwise inapproachable; a reality that views us as a metaphor of the Spirit itself, that attracts and inspires us.

The technique of a Martial Art, in order to be learnt, requires much effort, attention and constant improvement, until the complexity of the many components that take part in it can be converted into the simplicity of a unique feeling of our own action; until we get to the borderland between nature and Spirit. The Way towards this land is a gradual process, but the perception of such border is a sudden illumination.

There are more ways to get to that horizon, but in no moment of those paths will it be possible to disclose in advance the knowledge of the nature of that extreme experience, of that fall. No sensation, if not in brief flashes, will be similar to that sudden change. Once we come close to the edge, to the extreme limit, in the enigma of having to walk past without being able to desire it, we will fight in order to stay and to avoid to retreat from the edge of the abyss, until, with no will but that of being devoted to our own talent, we will reach the condition of dignity and correctness from which, by nature and necessity, the perfect fall will open up.

The final point of the Way, the Borderland, marks the access to an intimate space of the self, essential but non transmittable, a space of which the sense and the content are not perceptible but, since they are implicit in it, in the ultimate knowledge. Its invisibleness is the proof of its authenticity. To perceive such reality a consistent, ceaseless, self-consciousness of ourselves is necessary; a feeling which is able to re-establish the uniformity of the immediate acknowledgment of everyone's own self being, without history nor time. A space which is uniquely available for freedom and pure beauty, emancipated by the attempt of exploitation and speculation of the inhumanity which constantly lies in ambush.

Once form and interaction conform to each other we become complete (Kansei) and the union among technical knowledge, execution and awareness of the action can manifest itself. The will of acting, after such singular experience, will come to life from a preexistent condition of harmony (Mushin), and the action itself will take place because of a necessity, not because of a choice.

Attracted by, or pushed towards, an unknown reality, we wish for this push to last while, at the same time, we do not know its destiny. The mysterious place, that we cannot help but lean toward, is the only alive and present thing that holds us away from the darkness of a time that seems endless and from a scary, inconstant future. We are required to conquer that state of well being in which the "before" and the "after" fade away, where they become mute in a space created by a full "here" and "now", where nothing could replace joy.

In the horizon of the Way lies an object-less certainty, the end of the illusion; a place where the understanding cannot proceed through knowledge, and where it looks obvious that a reflection in the water is as real as the moon in the sky.

The Way and the method

"What can contrast concurs
And thanks to elements which differ
We obtain the best harmony"

Heraclitus

The true Way is the Way that dates back to the origins, that recomposes an aware look over what we are and over the truth of what is done. Pacing the Way corresponds to a transformation, to an exploration of our own inner nature.

A School must offer an ideal form, a model to which we can confront ourselves until its completion is reached, until the sense of unity that can melt the conflicts of the reason has been conquered, to rely on a deeper nature, where being human means being fully aware and responsible.

The teaching must communicate the notions to build both the ideal form and the dynamic reasons which satisfy the Principles at the base of the tradition. Each initial intention that parts from the objectives of the School will be obstructed and will need to conform to the rules indicated by the master and will have to aspire, from that moment, through technique and art, to the actual goal of the action. When the intention will correspond to the Original Motivation, the practice will have reached its purpose.

Method and inspiration

The possibility to unify technique and Spirit concerns the affinity among our own attitude and the activity we wish to perform. The first sign of such compatibility is aesthetic recall for the spaces, the figures and the tools that are utilized. If the attraction persists and lasts with time then the authenticity of that wire which connects the art to the essence of everyone's own root is plausible.

One other element that supports this correspondence is the interest and the passion for the true knowledge which is, along with all of its literature, the point of major attraction that, if well developed, produces the effects of a mental revolution. Without passion for the culture, the thinking will never reach the same level of the technical execution.

A True Technique has to match, as already mentioned, to the characteristics of the person and of the utilized tools. The adaption to these characteristics suggests, as first consideration, the presence of modifiable parts and non modifiable parts of the method, as we will see later on.

The adjustments to the modifiable parts have to fit in with the fundamental rules, and to maintain those balances and those sensations which allow a clear perception and a limpid mental state. Because of the gradual realizations of the single parts of the technical execution, we attempt to obtain, from their relationship, a shared awareness. And it is evident that a master needs to have, not only the theoretical knowledge, but also the knowledge, obtained through experience, of the Correct Shot. It is displeasing to witness that some teachers have a vague and approximate knowledge over the mental states topic, as if it were a program or a theme which does not require to be verified and to be continuously improved for its application, and who draw their affirmations from common sayings and citations of various kind, following what is seen as fashionable. Moreover, it is just based on this ability that a master should evaluate the skills of a pupil and should be able to individuate a mental condition which is aware of an instinctual execution that, even if operative, does not allow the subject to control the action they are performing.

The correct action is a non divided experience, built for a bunch of technical competences that ensure an actual correspondence among external reality and the fundamental space of the Self; it is a precious and rare possibility to reach the true purpose of the Way and to unite our own self being with the spirit of nature.

The following part is dedicated to the description of the evolution process of the method through practice. From the initial conditions, through the most common aspects of the apprenticeship, to the most advanced states of the experience.

The execution of the method

The severity of a method implies, in the first place, its communicability, namely the possibility to transmit it respecting its authenticity and efficacy. The content of a teaching must be communicated through gestures and words, so that who is listening or who is watching can reach, through a theorem of sensations, the same, shared experience.

Whichever the starting reason to a practice is, to best ensure the respect of the rules and of the teachings, a desire of improvement must follow such reason to make it possible for experience, knowledge and awareness to focus on a common purpose.

The aim of the practice consists of performing an action, perceived in its unity, following the rules of the technique. Ultimately, perceiving an action in its wholeness corresponds to a conscience of the self that can be lived on different levels and with different intensities. Surely the experience of acting knowingly produces the growth of such sensitivity that stabilizes itself more and more as the action responds to the method. The growth of such sensitivity allows a better, more conscious control of the action and leaves less space to the impulsive part of the movement helping a meticulous and reliable execution.

The deference towards the teacher is also an indispensable condition for a good learning. Who is teaching needs to know the method and to have experimented it in the facts, and even if the ultimate knowledge of this experience is impossible to communicate, what is communicable has a great importance. The progress, in fact, is based on the observation of simple indications and on the continuous attempt to truly accomplish them, going beyond the impulses and our own convictions, towards a special sensitivity that can make new cognitive schemes and perceptions possible.

The best that can be done is practicing following the rules and doing it consciously, for a long time and constantly, under the guide of a valuable master.

Fundamental stages of the method

- **Accomplish the correct form.** The correct form helps the clear perception of the action that we want to perform and, with such lucidity, it is possible to apply the control and keep the perception of the self together with the conscious action. The first act or chapter of the path of learning about the Way consists of setting ourselves out to listening and to a careful observation of the basic models which are pointed out by the master. The following effort involves the attempts of putting into practice the received instructions. It is now that the ability to actually perform the actions is evaluated. Imitation is the first phase, it consists of the technical ability to repeat a move or a form, learning, so, even a new order of sensorial relations. This does not only include the cognitive act, but also those issues that are the first stage to understand the new experience.

The path to accomplish the Way starts with an accurate and more and more sought after correspondence among the form that is being carried out and the rules pointed out by the Densho of the School. It is important to keep in mind that during this learning path the pupil, who does not know the final mental condition of the accomplishment of the Way yet, has to carefully evaluate whether the action he is performing conforms to the received dispositions, rather than venture in personal conclusions. This is, of course, about an effort, a continuous attention and an attempt that, even if correct, needs to be linked to the sensation of an unsure outcome.

Until the full realization of the shot, the effort involved in the research of the form and of the execution cannot be avoided, and these, even if matched with variability and uncertainty, remark the commitment of the pupil when he acts consciously, without giving in to the instinct.

- **Study of the parts and of their reciprocal relationship.** With repetition and continuous attempts we enforce the study of particulars making it possible to accord, every time, the single parts with the inevitable consequence of a continuous change of perceptions and knowledge. The instability and the mistakes will have to be accepted.

It goes without saying that only with the support of the master will these conditions be bearable, they will generally last for a long time. It is here that our personal qualities take part in the process, when it comes to the estimation of the perceptions and of their reliability. Thus the ability of the pupil to maintain a judgment without compromises and the confidence in their own abilities. A determinate perception corresponds to a certain form and once the form is defined as correct, the correspondent perception is confirmed becoming a sensitive internal orientation signal.

Consequently, applying the practical instruction, piece by piece, a series of analytic judgments and orientation signals, that will oppose to the insistence of the instinct, can be created.

Moving from this first experience, through continuous tests, we will progress to more advanced situations. The focus of these paths or gradual passages is that of understanding the single movements to then unite them. And from elements conserved and learnt as partial processes, we will move on to an overall action that is as stable as it is free from the process of imagination of the action that has got to be performed. If this will be, the sensations will end up back together in a unique moving body, perceived as a unique and indistinguishable form.

- **Unified and conscious execution.** The top of the process is when the single parts are united in a way not to elude the compactness of the whole in which they reside. It is like this that the correct action can take place. Keeping in mind that if we think of particulars as independent elements, the consciousness of the action in its whole gets ruined and the general balance is compromised. It is all about realizing a pure perception without images, an automatism that we are aware of. In the correct action there are no moves which are performed unconsciously, nor controlled impulses that set up a condition that can be defined hostile to the free and balanced expression of the energies.

This moment of mental growth, which sets itself apart thanks to the natural actions consciously experienced and in the detriment of instinctive behaviors and impulsive acts, represents the benefit that we expect by practicing a Way. In this moment the attempts to improve the particulars by restoring a balance which is continually evolving, will be alternated with a unitary and more fluid action, testing ground of the achieved coordination level.

Obviously, both the teaching and that the considerations of the practitioner have a fundamental role in order to avoid instinctive actions and premature automatisms. The attempt to interpret the lived experience is also a measure of one's personal attitudes and abilities. But only when the execution will derive from a clear mental situation will it be possible to observe and distinguish it in its particulars and to accurately perform it. Inside of this forge of transformations, knowledge and disappointments, the ups and downs of a mainly unforeseeable path alternate themselves. The awareness is the conscience enriched by a true experience. And if this experience has got the prerogative of an artistic or virtuous act, then the personality potentiates itself with unique values and with a more stable condition of mental presence. The will can then correspond to the method, where form and energy are adapted to the intention that moves them. Those who have realized the experience of a complete and correct technique, can take advantage, in case they want to cover the role of the teacher, of this knowledge. In fact, the ability to repossess such experience, also finding a balance with the internal lived which corresponds to it, makes a non common sensitivity available, which is able to guide and

orientate itself, effortlessly, being loyal
to the laws of the method.

In conclusion, even if for a long time the study will be limited to the investigation and will insist on certain particulars of the form or of the single movements, in the end anyway, the action will have to be unified and to derive from a unique intention. Forms and sensations have to depend on the unique and original motivation. The executers, while perceiving themselves, also need to be aware, in each phase, of the reason of their action. This is the important result of our search: a determination that stays alive until the conclusion of the action. For the duration of the learning time, the execution will be arbitrary, insecure and often wrong and will necessarily need to be assisted and directed by one of the masters of the School. The pupil has to give up on personal decisions and initiative while the master decides and watches over everything so that the trial responds to the established technical Principles. In the end, the pupil will always have to act trying to conform the action to the received teachings. Himself, with the correct application of the rules, will be in the best condition to reach the true purpose of the practice: that visibility and clarity indispensable to control each movement of their action. It is then that the moves will take place with the smallest possible effort and without uncertainties, and the mind, from the beginning, will guide an action of which knows the end. With the Clear Vision of the action even the imperfections will be caught, and they will be solved in order to reach the perfect action. In the Enlightened Mind the Harmony can manifest itself even in the imperfection of the action.

"The virtue shines, the ability is not important"

[Hakuin]

The imperative law of each Martial Art says that the action has as its purpose to act consciously and hit the enemy with the maximum efficacy and simplicity. This is possible thanks to a True Technique and to a quiet and perceptive mind.

Rhythm

HYŌSHI
Harmonize tools, technique and mind

We often act casually and in a confusing way, while the tension increases, in the attempt to govern the moves. Other times, instead, when the intention is followed by an easy execution, suddenly the Clear Light of awareness and the benefit of a natural rhythm reveal themselves.

This state of inconstancy and unpredictable situations derive, in the first place, from a poor knowledge of the performed action or from an uncertain motivation which lacks the unity of the topic; the expression gets lost in a discordance of gestures and sensations and the action follows a rhythm that obeys to unknown forces.

Thus, form and perception are the topics to develop. With a bigger knowledge and discipline it will be easier to re establish the harmonic and natural rhythm. The explorer of the Way will have to work on their technique and the experience of perceptions and sensation; it is like this that they will be able to participate with more consciousness of the execution, in which they will learn to be, where appropriated, actor and observer. They will need to progress in order to distinguish better and better these two states: the intention and the listening, until they know in depth the rules of the alternation of these two elements or states that, like a breath, are the tide between the I and the concrete; a clear vision of the consonance among the rule and our own sensations. Being conscious of this breath is the Art and its evolution accompanies and guides the practitioner of the Way.

Natural action

"In the instant of separation, your heart is without thoughts, without wishes"

[Heki Danjo]

If the action that corresponds to the intention is a harmonic action, then it is lived consciously.

The correct execution, with the full awareness of the action that is being performed, covers an elevated ethical value, thanks to an art, or better, to a presence that refers to a deeper existential meaning and which makes it shine through.

The best and most effective action must be free from thoughts and evaluations of any kind and it needs to be carried out through a conscious automatism, in harmony with the natural principles. And it is just because of this proximity with the nature, that it has as focus and resolution element the harmony between the complementary strengths of Yin and Yang, that the technique becomes art.

And through art, the conviction and then the certainty that the Way can reach the highest values of the spirit are strengthened.

> *"The butterfly flies*
> *Without any desire*
> *In this world"*
>
> [Issa Kobayashi]

The conquest of the real

"Make it possible for me to always be able to walk before the wind, that the fearful rabbit does not escape before my arrival"

[Navajo]

Realizing the Way is the conquest, which is in need of a continuous renewal. Along the Way the web of new experiences comes to view bit by bit, as if it came out from behind the hump of an unstoppable progress. It is a source of new sensitivity for the restless conquest of the present and of the real, since it seems that in the material world of the Spirit achievement does not exist, this world looks as if it were stable and definitive, as if it did not need to be reaffirmed or maintained effective, through forces of which the nature is mostly unknown. The attempt to establish and acquire these experiences, increases the need of a better consciousness and determination, also translatable in sensitivity and attitude.

Sensitivity and precision of the technical execution, build each other up mutually. Balance and movement quality help a mental state of more intense perceptive clarity. While, how to feed and strengthen the character, pertains to the way in which the mind recognizes the proof of actual reality, ignoring false and illusory perceptions.

Distinguishing between the real and the thought of is at the base of the growth process. Growing up inside of the Way is a process that regenerates spontaneously our quality of being sympathetic and aware of the world we live in, and it allows us, if we want to see it this way, to retrace and rebuild the tissue of the events of the past and of those unresolved parts of that story of which we are undeletable and indivisible substance. The quality of the perception is the principal ingredient of this renewing art and it is the mental space in which the perceived is translated, or better, decoded, to then be used in a creative or evolution scheme. Once we are aware of the object of the perfection it is determinant to be able to estimate and recognize the value and the proof of actual reality, distancing ourselves from false perceptions

46

which depend on emotional and moral disorders and to these are connected.

The evolution of the being, its important transformation can be traced in depth. Just this transformation of the thoughts, from thoughts that do not follow and order to ordered thoughts, is the base of the internal progress of the person. The retrieval of this ordered state is a natural, non conditioned answer of thoughts and acts that already have a logical development inside of themselves, and which mute effortless. It is this new way of being, real and present, that, modeling itself, takes part in the improvement of everything it is surrounded by. With repeated visions of the true essence of things (Kenshō) the constant of the wise "nature of Buddha" gradually gets established. Sensitivity, which grows while processing along the Way, can then generate an interior mutation, with the vision of a new place. Progress, when it is about this place, is hardly perceptible, but for particular situations or with facts that reach and touch that nucleus from which, conscious or not, emerges each new answer.

Therefore, we have to practice in order to improve, to remark with more and more strength the consistence of the present, perceptive tissue, since actually real element. The emotional task of the past, unresolved experiences changes and gets weaker, and proceeding, reduces itself to simple factors and annotations without any activity; assumption for a clear listening of the self and of the reasons that move desires and intentions.

The conquest of the real is a direct perception of "that which is", a sight free from conditioning and from emotional dimming. Thinking evolves to a thinking which is a stranger to time. And time, which actually lapses, is the time of the healing.

I do not know how far and if the quantity, the weight or the music of my individual track, is enough to a true comprehension, since I do not have any other way of conceiving this, if not mine; and I do not know if it can be shared in a common experience where each discussed part leads to a unique root of truth. I think, anyway, that whatever is written or told by the heart, beyond opinions, always holds in itself a little bit of truth that, no matter how thin or light its voice is, will be understood and maybe shared, if the listening is sincere.

Perfection

KANZEN - Completeness – KAN - Aware
Unification

In the fullness of a vast consciousness, everything is realer, and the large number of possibilities and connections among the single parts turns off the gross distinctions connected to a superficial observation of a small world. Being able to grasp the greatness with a sensitive and unified vision avoids the effort of having to be identifiable and persuaded to be worth, in a living space full and suffocating of density and fragments which require, in order to to make sense, to be defined, overcome and brought to the next level. And it is in such a limited and narrow way that, in the attempt to find an overall reason, we move away from the present, looking for a kind of knowledge that will never be more than a self-conviction. Who has already obeyed to themselves cannot see the truth of the present.

The Way is a constant renewal towards this completeness of vision, and the research to recreate, with every step and in every occasion, the harmony of the thought and of the moment, has no end.

One can never stop learning the art of being present. Each moment is a complete revolution, a rebirth and the new conquest of an absolute freedom; and this is possible only in the absence of any effort, in being wholly, simply ourselves.

Fundamental ethic

Perception and experience of the real

The correct action is an action free of judgments, beliefs and cultures. It is an action that draws its naturalness from the harmony of perceptions and from a sensitivity which is capable of giving space and echo to the diffusion of such harmony. A clearer and clearer perception of reality, that gives life to behaviors free of tensions and fake appearances, towards a deeper awareness of their moral meaning.

Being aware of the present condition means perceiving the presuppositions of an action and the values connected to it; perceiving, deep inside, a different beauty that, in the indecipherable and intuitive connection to a superior reality, could produce a constant tendency, a strength that can trace the Way to which we should dedicate each action and thought. Being always present to ourselves and stick with this conviction as we would with a possible space, even if actually with a reality in many ways inexplicable.

It means conquering, like this, a place where beauty is spread without limitations and without attraction, stranger to the reason, empty from thoughts and memory. A perfect space where the mind sees everything while unwilling to look at anything. And where perceive or being perceived makes no difference.

Yūgen

MONO NO AWARE

Aesthetic and Feeling
Being conscious of things recognizing their meaning and their function.

The clearer and the more detailed the knowledge of a method, the bigger the level of knowledge that one has of it during its application. Knowledge is a progress of the quality and functionality of human activities. There is, then, another way of interpreting the human progress, that of art, of poetry, that of letting things flow according to harmony and nature. A creativity that manifests itself out of our control and often out of our will. This is just its biggest quality, in the rhythm that shines through despite everything.

If in the first example evolving means being aware of the world we live in, in the example of the floating world, of harmony and poetry evolving seems to be an unknown beauty, that could bring us back to a knowledge beyond rational thinking.

After all, I believe that the quality of a Way consists of making the union of the two necessary progresses possible through the Way itself, two progresses that complete each other and give each other strength reciprocally. At first, through the knowledge of a technique, one becomes conscious of the reasons to the action. Then, when from this comprehension we can perfect the subject, until it perfectly corresponds to its aim, we can reach that art of the harmonious nature; but now, with the full knowledge and with a vision of nature and beauty, filled with the awareness of the Spirit. The automatism, at the end of such process, will be bright and visible.

This, for me, is the value of the Way. Not only a journey towards virtue and the sense of life, it is a path towards the truth. I am sure this is the reason of being an individual: in having to transform an endless, emotionless, cosmic beauty into a living presence. And the first step is being conscious, since nothing can lose what touches the free space of the mind; what awakens in the present.

Realization
JITSUGEN

The correct action in the Martial Art
*"Identical to the reflection of the moon in the water, is
the vision of the reflection of the action in the mind"*

[Urakami Sakae]

Art of the knowledge
Awareness is the state of perception of a
known action, united to the sensation of the
self. From which we understand that the
comprehension of the technique is essential
in order to perform a conscious action.

The correct execution, with the full
awareness of the action that is being performed, acquires an elevated ethic value
thanks to an art, or better, to a presence that
it allows to come through, and it hints to a
deeper meaning of being aware and free. The
correct technique turns into moral correctness, in wider words, nobility of the behavior
and respect for life itself.

Technique, when it is the True Technique, has as aim and resolution element the

harmony between strength and elasticity. And a perfect natural execution can be a way of searching and knowing deeply the connection between person and nature. Only knowing how and why the action is happening can we know it more intimately. On the contrary, not knowing how the single parts of the shot follow each other or fit together, will lead to an instinctive action, whose darkness will leave little to the value of the experience.

Zen practice

The Norm - Strict Rules - The Tradition

Following the tradition of the Zen practice, I would like to treat the topic of the Way attempting to establish the characteristics and peculiarities that the practice of any Way or art should have in order to be defined "authentic Zen practice". Along with these, I would like to specify which are the skills and attitudes that the practitioners need in order to be called "true pupil" or "true practitioner of the Way."

Zen practice requires total and unconditional acceptance of the rules and the dispositions issued by the instructor, the school and its authorized representatives. The pupils must follow the dispositions and put them into practice, even though they may not understand the motivations to such rules. They are allowed to ask questions to reach a better understanding of the rules but it is forbidden to discuss them or their validity.

The Zen practitioner must study the topics and practice the techniques extensively while attempting to understand in depth the norms, the concepts and the ideas which form the basics of the values and the truth of the Way.

Working and mastering only certain parts of a Zen practice or a martial art is not enough to ensure its survival. All aspects should be investigated, understood, taken care of and preserved with great determination.

The pupil is required to listen and to put the teachings into practice attempting to find the correct form, the precise action and the most effective way. Loyalty and sincerity are not enough in the absence of passion for the truth. Nothing could ever replace the curiosity concerning the comprehension of our own nature and the research of higher energies and entities, along with their perceivable signs, and of the voice and the presence. All of this in order to be motivated to undertake a lifelong path.

Even though, while walking the Way, the actions might be imperfect and the thoughts and knowledge might be uncertain, the objectives must be honest and the will to respect every rule must be perfect until the condition of the correct Way of the Eightfold Path is reached. The latter refers to Straight Perception (*sight of the correct way of thinking*) and Straight Interpretation of the Perception (*comprehension*); Straight Expression through the use of the *word* and of the *action* (aesthetics); Straight choice of conduct (*ethics*); Straight execution, careful, precise and aware (*effort, consciousness, concentration*).

Zen is support and extinction of every phenomenon, it is the non-separation and, therefore, it is perfect equality. It is a place where there cannot be more beauty than that which we can perceive nor more pain than that which we can bear. Zen is *order*, that makes pain, illness and the end of life beautiful.

Zen is death. It is its living face.

The act free from impulsive forms
It is like the dark space invaded by light

Three Dragons in flight

*In the enlightened mind, harmony and
clear vision, they can also manifest in
imperfection of form and action.*

*Furthermore, the correct form or the
correct action, it may not lead to a clear
view or an enlightened mind.*

Enlightenment is a gift

IL°MELETO

Production of literary
Casa Zen
Center for study and conversation

Established in November 2000
in Pomara fraction of Gazzuolo
(the Gonzaga apple orchard)
(MN) - Italy

Author, *Elia Bardinero*
Pseudonym of Giuseppe Costa

First edition
September 2019

IL°MELETO

Index of illustrations

Poems and writings cited, of:

Bibliography of Giuseppe Costa
(*Pseudonym* , Elia Bardinero)

He has written and published:
Various publications, general and monographic, philosophy, poetry and pictorial art history and Italian sculpture.

"Tre libri sulla Via", *March 2017*
"La Via alla Virtù", *2015 [internal publication]*

To receive detailed information about the bibliography about the author, make a request to the Archive "Scuola delle quattro Foglie". [*Giuseppecst6@gmail.com*]

With the Pseudonym of Elia Bardinero, he has published:
"Sfingi e Cariatidi – Metodo e Meditazione", *January 2018*
  *(Literary production of the "*IL°*MELETO")*

and will publish:
"Voci d'acque", *2019*
"Piccolo trattato sulla vastità della mente".
"Monaci".

Biographical notes of professional activity:

Art critic, since 1982. He has worked profession-ally for public and private institutions. Writer and publicist (at the Genoa branch of "*Il Giornale*").
From 1997 to 2006, he collaborated on the Catalog of "*Italian Painters of the Nineteenth Century*" Ed. Allemandi.

From 1980 to 1982, in Shanghai, he followed the teaching of Ch'an Master, Ten Zhi Yuan .

Since 1996 he has been a member of the Scientific Council of the *Ligurian Center for Oriental Studies in Genoa* (CELSO) and a professor at the same Institute until 2003, in the Japanese section of the Asian Studies Department.

In 1997, he joined the group of teachers of the Heki Ryū Insai Ha (Kyudō), directed by the teacher Toshio Mori, of the *University of Tsukuba*.

He is a master in the practice of the Zen Conversation (Mondō), in Novellara (RE) and at the Practice Center "*Casa Zen*" in Pomara (MN).

Born in Italy.

The author at the Bisiolo stable
'Conversation Room'
"Free Community Zen" Asola, 1997

notes ___________________________________

notes _______________________________

notes ____

Publication manager:
Giuseppe Costa

IL°MELETO